The Constitution of
The State of Rhode Island:
A Quick Reference Guide

Bootblack Budget Books
Copyright 2018 @
ISBN-13: 978-1721893638
ISBN-10: 1721893636

Contents:

Section 1. Right to Make and Alter Constitution - Constitution Obligatory Upon All

Section 2. Laws for Good of Whole - Burdens to be Equally Distributed - Due Process - Equal Protection - Discrimination - No Right to Abortion Granted

Section 3. Freedom of Religion

Section 4. Slavery Prohibited - Slavery Shall not be Permitted in this State

Section 5. Entitlement to Remedies for Injuries and Wrongs - Right to Justice

Section 6. Search and Seizure

Section 7. Requirement of Presentment or Indictment - Information by Attorney-General - Grand Juries - Double Jeopardy

Section 8. Bail, Fines and Punishments

Section 9. Right to bail - Habeas Corpus

Section 10. Rights of Accused Persons in Criminal Proceedings

Section 11. Relief of Debtors from Prison

Section 12. Ex Post Facto Laws - Laws Impairing Obligation of Contract

Section 13. Self-Crimination

No person in a court of common law shall be compelled to give self-criminating evidence.

Section 14. Presumption Of Innocence - Securing Accused Persons

Every person being presumed innocent, until pronounced guilty by the law, no act of severity which is not necessary to secure an accused person shall be permitted.

Section 15. Trial by Jury

The right of trial by jury shall remain inviolate. In civil cases the general assembly may fix the size of the petit jury at less than twelve but not less than six.

Section 16. Compensation for Taking of Private Property for Public Use - Regulation of Fishery Rights and Shore Privileges Not Public Taking

Section 17. Fishery Rights - Shore Privileges - Preservation of Natural Resources

Section 18. Subordination of Military to Civil Authority - Martial Law

Section 19. Quartering of soldiers

Section 20. Freedom of Press

Section 21. Right to Assembly - Redress of Grievances - Freedom of Speech

Section 22. Right to Bear Arms

Section 23. Rights of Victims of Crime

Section 24. Rights not Enumerated - State Rights not Dependent on Federal Rights

Article II: Suffrage – Page 29

Article V: Distribution of Powers – Page 38

Section 1. Distribution of Powers

Article VIII: Senate – Page 48

Section 1. Composition

Section 2. Lieutenant Governor to be Presiding Officer until 2003

Section 3. Repealed

Section 4. Repealed

Article IX: Executive Power – Page 49

Section 16. Limitation on State Spending. [Effective July 1,2007 until July 1, 2012]

Section 16. Limitation on State Spending

Section 17. Budget Reserve Account

Article XIV: Constitutional Amendments and Revision – Page 65

Section 1. Procedure for Proposing and Approving Amendments

Section 2. Constitutional Conventions

Article XV: General Transition – Page 66

Section 1. Rights and Duties of Public Bodies Unaffected – Continuation of Laws, Ordinances, Regulations and Rules

Section 2. Validity of Bonds, Debts, Contracts, Suits, Actions, and Rights of Actions Continued

Section 3. Continuation of Office Holders

Section 4. Implementing Legislation for Article III, Sections 7 and 8, and Article IV, section 10

Preamble:

In order effectually to secure the religious and political freedom established by our venerated ancestors, and to preserve the same for our posterity, we do declare that the essential and unquestionable rights and principles hereinafter mentioned shall be established, maintained, and preserved, and shall be of paramount obligation in all legislative, judicial and executive proceedings.

ARTICLE I: DECLARATION OF CERTAIN CONSTITUTIONAL RIGHTS AND PRINCIPLES

Section 1. Right to Make and Alter Constitution - Constitution Obligatory Upon All

In the words of the Father of his Country, we declare that "the basis of our political systems is the right of the people to make and alter their constitutions of government; but that the constitution which at any time exists, till changed by an explicit and authentic act of the whole people, is sacredly obligatory upon all."

Section 2. Laws for Good of Whole - Burdens to be Equally Distributed - Due Process - Equal Protection - Discrimination - No Right to Abortion Granted

All free governments are instituted for the protection, safety, and happiness of the people. All laws, therefore, should be made for the good of the whole; and the burdens of the state ought to be fairly distributed among its citizens. No person shall be deprived of life, liberty or property without due process of law, nor shall any person be denied equal protection of the laws. No otherwise qualified person shall, solely by reason of race, gender or handicap be subject to discrimination by the state, its agents or any person or entity doing business with the state. Nothing in this section shall be construed to grant or secure any right relating to abortion or the funding thereof.

Section 3. Freedom of Religion

Whereas Almighty God hath created the mind free; and all attempts to influence it by temporal punishments or burdens, or by civil incapacitations, tend to beget habits of hypocrisy and meanness; and whereas a principal object of our venerable ancestors, in their migration to this country and their settlement of this state, was, as they expressed it, to hold forth a lively experiment that a flourishing civil state may stand and be best maintained with full liberty in religious concernments; we, therefore, declare that no person shall be compelled to frequent or to support any religious worship, place, or ministry whatever, except in fulfillment of such person's voluntary contract; nor enforced, restrained, molested, or burdened in body or goods; nor disqualified from holding any office; nor otherwise suffer on account of such person's religious belief; and that every person shall be free to worship God according to the dictates of such person's conscience, and to profess and by argument to maintain such person's opinion in matters of religion; and that the same shall in no wise diminish, enlarge, or affect the civil capacity of any person.

Section 4. Slavery Prohibited - Slavery Shall not be Permitted in this State

Section 5. Entitlement to Remedies for Injuries and Wrongs - Right to Justice

Every person within this state ought to find a certain remedy, by having recourse to the laws, for all injuries or wrongs which may be received in one's person, property, or character. Every person ought to obtain right and justice freely, and without purchase, completely and without denial; promptly and without delay; conformably to the laws.

Section 6. Search and Seizure

The right of the people to be secure in their persons, papers and possessions, against unreasonable searches and seizures, shall not be violated; and no warrant shall issue, but on complaint in writing, upon probable cause, supported by oath or affirmation, and describing as nearly as may be, the place to be searched and the persons or things to be seized.

Section 7. Requirement of Presentment or Indictment -
Information by Attorney-General - Grand Juries - Double
Jeopardy

Except in cases of impeachment, or in cases arising in the land or
naval forces, or in the militia when in actual service in time of
war or public danger, no person shall be held to answer for any
offense which is punishable by death or by imprisonment for life
unless on presentment or indictment by a grand jury, and no
person shall be held to answer for any other felony unless on
presentment or indictment by a grand jury or on information in
writing signed by the attorney-general or one of the attorney-
general's designated assistants, as the general assembly may
provide and in accordance with procedures enacted by the
general assembly. The general assembly may authorize the
impaneling of grand juries with authority to indict for offenses
committed any place within the state and it may provide that
more than one grand jury may sit simultaneously within a county.
No person shall be subject for the same offense to be twice put
in jeopardy. Nothing contained in this article shall be construed
as in any wise impairing the inherent common law powers of the
grand jury.

Section 8. Bail, Fines and Punishments

Excessive bail shall not be required, nor excessive fines imposed,
nor cruel punishments inflicted; and all punishments ought to be
proportioned to the offense.

Section 9. Right to bail - Habeas Corpus

All persons imprisoned ought to be bailed by sufficient surety,
unless for offenses punishable by imprisonment for life, or for
offenses involving the use or threat of use of a dangerous
weapon by one already convicted of such an offense or already
convicted of an offense punishable by imprisonment for life, or
for an offense involving the unlawful sale, distribution,
manufacturer, delivery, or possession with intent to manufacture,

sell, distribute or deliver any controlled substance or by possession or by a controlled substance punishable by imprisonment for ten (10) years or more, when the proof of guilt is evident or the presumption great. Nothing in this section shall be construed to confer a right to bail, pending appeal of a conviction. The privilege of the writ of habeas corpus shall not be suspended, unless when in cases of rebellion or invasion, the public safety shall require it; nor ever without the authority of the general assembly.

Section 10. Rights of Accused Persons in Criminal Proceedings

In all criminal prosecutions, accused persons shall enjoy the right to a speedy and public trial, by an impartial jury; to be informed of the nature and cause of the accusation, to be confronted with the witnesses against them, to have compulsory process for obtaining them in their favor, to have the assistance of counsel in their defense, and shall be at liberty to speak for themselves; nor shall they be deprived of life, liberty, or property, unless by the judgment of their peers, or the law of the land.

Section 11. Relief of Debtors from Prison

The person of a debtor, when there is not strong presumption of fraud, ought not to be continued in prison, after such person shall have delivered up property for the benefit of said person's creditors, in such manner as shall be prescribed by law.

Section 12. Ex Post Facto Laws - Laws Impairing Obligation of Contract

No ex post facto law, or law impairing the obligation of contracts, shall be passed.

Section 13. Self-Crimination

No person in a court of common law shall be compelled to give self-criminating evidence.

Section 14. Presumption Of Innocence - Securing Accused Persons

Every person being presumed innocent, until pronounced guilty by the law, no act of severity which is not necessary to secure an accused person shall be permitted.

Section 15. Trial by Jury

The right of trial by jury shall remain inviolate. In civil cases the general assembly may fix the size of the petit jury at less than twelve but not less than six.

Section 16. Compensation for Taking of Private Property for Public Use - Regulation of Fishery Rights and Shore Privileges Not Public Taking

Private property shall not be taken for public uses, without just compensation. The powers of the state and of its municipalities to regulate and control the use of land and waters in the furtherance of the preservation, regeneration, and restoration of the natural environment, and in furtherance of the protection of the rights of the people to enjoy and freely exercise the rights of fishery and the privileges of the shore, as those rights and duties are set forth in section 17, shall be an exercise of the police powers of the state, shall be liberally construed, and shall not be deemed to be a public use of private property.

Section 17. Fishery Rights - Shore Privileges - Preservation of Natural Resources

The people shall continue to enjoy and freely exercise all the rights of fishery, and the privileges of the shore, to which they have been heretofore entitled under the charter and usages of this state, including but not limited to fishing from the shore, the gathering of seaweed, leaving the shore to swim in the sea and passage along the shore; and they shall be secure in their rights to the use and enjoyment of the natural resources of the state with due regard for the preservation of their values; and it shall be the duty of the general assembly to provide for the conservation of the air, land, water, plant, animal, mineral and other natural resources of the state, and to adopt all means necessary and proper by law to protect the natural environment of the people of the state by providing adequate resource planning for the control and regulation of the use of the natural resources of the state and for the preservation, regeneration and restoration of the natural environment of the state.

Section 18. Subordination of Military to Civil Authority - Martial Law

The military shall be held in strict subordination to the civil authority. And the law martial shall be used and exercised in such cases only as occasion shall necessarily require.

Section 19. Quartering of soldiers

No soldier shall be quartered in any house in time of peace, without the consent of the owner; nor, in time of war, but in manner to be prescribed by law.

Section 20. Freedom of Press

The liberty of the press being essential to the security of freedom in a state, any person may publish sentiments on any subject, being responsible for the abuse of that liberty; and in all trials for libel, both civil and criminal, the truth, unless published from malicious motives, shall be sufficient defense to the person charged.

Section 21. Right to Assembly - Redress of Grievances - Freedom of Speech

The citizens have a right in a peaceable manner to assembly for their common good, and to apply to those invested with the powers of government, for redress of grievances, or for other purposes, by petition, address, or remonstrance. No law abridging the freedom of speech shall be enacted.

Section 22. Right to Bear Arms

The right of the people to keep and bear arms shall not be infringed.

Section 23. Rights of Victims of Crime

A victim of crime shall, as a matter of right, be treated by agents of the state with dignity, respect and sensitivity during all phases of the criminal justice process. Such person shall be entitled to receive, from the perpetrator of the crime, financial compensation for any injury or loss caused by the perpetrator of the crime, and shall receive such other compensation as the state may provide. Before sentencing, a victim shall have the right to address the court regarding the impact which the perpetrator's conduct has had upon the victim.

Section 24. Rights not Enumerated - State Rights not Dependent on Federal Rights

The enumeration of the foregoing rights shall not be construed to impair or deny others retained by the people. The rights guaranteed by this Constitution are not dependent on those guaranteed by the Constitution of the United States.

ARTICLE II: SUFFRAGE

Section 1. Persons Entitled to Vote

Every citizen of the United States of the age of eighteen years or over who has had residence and home in this state for thirty days next preceding the time of voting, who has resided thirty days in the town or city from which such citizen desires to vote, and whose name shall be registered at least thirty days next preceding the time of voting as provided by law, shall have the right to vote for all offices to be elected and on all questions submitted to the electors, except that no person who has been lawfully adjudicated to be non compos mentis shall be permitted to vote. No person who is incarcerated in a correctional facility upon a felony conviction shall be permitted to vote until such person is discharged from the facility. Upon discharge, such person's right to vote shall be restored. The general assembly may provide by law for shorter state and local residence requirements to vote for electors for president and vice president of the United States.

Section 2. Nomination of Candidates — Voter Registration — Absentee Voting — Conduct of Elections — Residency

The general assembly shall provide by law for the nomination of candidates; for a uniform system of permanent registration of voters; for the exemption from such registration of persons in the active service of the nation and their families absent from the state because of such service, and, in time of war, members of the Merchant Marine; for absentee and shut in voting; for the time, manner and place of conducting elections; for the prevention of abuse, corruption and fraud in voting; and may define by law residence for voting purposes, but no person shall acquire such residence merely by being stationed or assigned in this state in the active service of the United States.

ARTICLE III: QUALIFICATION FOR OFFICE

Section 1. Qualified Electors

No person shall hold any civil office unless that person be a qualified elector for such office.

Section 2. Disqualification Upon Conviction or Plea of Nolo Contendere – Re-Qualification Following Sentence, Probation or Parole

An elector shall be disqualified as a candidate for elective or appointive state or local office or from holding such office if such elector has been convicted of or plead nolo contendere to a felony or if such elector has been convicted or plead nolo contendere to a misdemeanor resulting in a jail sentence of six months or more, either suspended or to be served. Such elector shall not, once so convicted, attain or return to any office until three years after the date of completion of such sentence and of probation or parole.

Section 3. Oath of General Officers

All general officers shall take the following engagement before they act in their respective offices, to wit: You being by the free vote of the electors of this state of Rhode Island and Providence Plantations, elected unto the place of do solemnly swear (or, affirm) to be true and faithful unto this state, and to support the Constitution of this state and of the United States; that you will faithfully and impartially discharge all the duties of your aforesaid office to the best of your abilities, according to law:

So help you God.

 Or:

This affirmation you make and give upon the peril of the penalty of perjury.

Section 4. Oath of General Assembly Members, Judges, and other Officers

The members of the general assembly, the judges of all the courts, and all other officers, both civil and military, shall be bound by oath or affirmation to support this Constitution, and the Constitution of the United States.

Section 5. Administration of Oaths

The oath or affirmation shall be administered to the governor, lieutenant governor, senators, and representatives by the secretary of state, or, in the absence of the secretary of state by the attorney-general. The secretary of state, attorney-general, and general treasurer shall be engaged by the governor, or by a justice of the supreme court.

Section 6. Holding of Offices Under other Governments – Senators and Representatives not to Hold other Appointed Offices Under State Government

No person holding any office under the government of the United States, or of any other state or country, shall act as a general officer or as a member of the general assembly, unless at the time of taking such engagement that person shall have resigned the office under such government; and if any general officer, senator, representative, or judge shall, after election and engagement, accept any appointment under any other government, the office under this shall be immediately vacated; but this restriction shall not apply to any person appointed to take deposition or acknowledgment of deeds, or other legal instruments, by the authority of any other state or country. No senator or representative shall, during the time for which he or she was elected, be appointed to any state office, board, commission or other state or quasi-public entity exercising executive power under the laws of this state, and no person holding any executive office or serving as a member of any board, commission or other state or quasi-public entity exercising executive power under the laws of this state shall be a member of the senate or the house of representatives during his or her continuance in such office.

Section 7. Ethical Conduct

The people of the state of Rhode Island believe that public officials and employees must adhere to the highest standards of ethical conduct, respect the public trust and the rights of all persons, be open, accountable and responsive, avoid the appearance of impropriety and not use their position for private gain or advantage. Such persons shall hold their positions during good behavior.

Section 8. Ethics Commission – Code of Ethics

The general assembly shall establish an independent non-partisan ethics commission which shall adopt a code of ethics including, but not limited to, provisions on conflicts of interest, confidential information, use of position, contracts with government agencies and financial disclosure. All elected and appointed officials and employees of state and local government, of boards, commissions and agencies shall be subject to the code of ethics. The ethics commission shall have the authority to investigate violations of the code of ethics and to impose penalties, as provided by law; and the commission shall have the power to remove from office officials who are not subject to impeachment.

ARTICLE IV: ELECTIONS AND CAMPAIGN FINANCE

Section 1. Election and Terms of Governor, Lieutenant Governor, Secretary of State, Attorney-General, General Treasurer, and General Assembly Members

The governor, lieutenant governor, secretary of state, attorney-general, general treasurer shall be elected on the Tuesday after the first Monday in November, quadrennially commencing A.D. 1994, and every four (4) years thereafter, and shall severally hold their offices, subject to recall as provided herein, for four (4) years from the first Tuesday of January next succeeding their election and until their successors are elected and qualified. No person shall serve consecutively in the same general office for more than two (2) full terms, excluding any partial term of less than two (2) years previously served. The senators and representatives in the general assembly shall be elected on the Tuesday after the first Monday in November, biennially in even numbered years, and shall severally hold their offices for two (2) years from the first Tuesday of January next succeeding their election and until their successors are elected and qualified. Recall is authorized in the case of a general officer who has been indicted or informed against for a felony, convicted of a misdemeanor, or against whom a finding of probable cause of violation of the code of ethics has been made by the ethics commission. Recall shall not, however be instituted at any time during the first six (6) months or the last year of an individual's term of office. Such a recall may be instituted by filing with the state board of elections an application for issuance of a recall petition against said general officer which is signed by duly qualified electors equal to three percent (3%) of the total number of votes cast at the last preceding general election for that office. If, upon verification, the application is determined to contain signatures of the required number of electors, the state board of elections shall issue a recall petition for circulation amongst the electors of the state. Within ninety (90) days of issuance, recall petitions containing the signatures of duly qualified electors constituting fifteen percent (15%) of the total number of votes cast in the last preceding general election for said office must be filed with the state board of elections. The signatures to the application and to the recall petition need not all be on one (1) sheet of paper, but each such application and petition must contain an identical statement naming the person to be recalled, the general office held by said person, and the grounds for such recall set forth in a statement of one hundred (100) words or less approved by the board of elections. Each signatory must set forth his or her signature as it appears on the voting list, the date of signing, and his or her place of residence. The person witnessing the signatures of each elector on said petition must sign a statement under oath on said sheet attesting that the signatures thereon are genuine and were signed in his or her presence. If the requisite number of signatures are not obtained within said ninety (90) days period, the recall effort shall terminate. Upon verification of the requisite number of signatures, a special election shall be scheduled at which the issue of removing said office holder and the grounds therefor shall be placed before the electors of the state. If a majority of those voting support removal of said office holder, the office shall be immediately declared vacant and shall be filled in accordance with the constitution and laws of the state. The person so removed shall not be eligible to fill the unexpired portion of the term of office. The general assembly shall provide by statute for implementation of the recall process.

Section 2. Election by Plurality

In all elections held by the people for state, city, town, ward or district officers, the person or candidate receiving the largest number of votes cast shall be declared elected.

Section 3. Filling Vacancy Caused by Death, Removal, Refusal to Serve, or Incapacity of Elected Officers -- Election when no Candidate Receives Plurality

When the governor-elect shall die, remove from the state, refuse to serve; become insane, or be otherwise incapacitated, the lieutenant governor-elect shall be qualified as governor at the beginning of the term for which the governor was elected. When both the governor and lieutenant governor-elect, or either the lieutenant governor, secretary of state, attorney-general, or general treasurer-elect, are so incapacitated, or when there has been a failure to elect any one or more of the officers mentioned in this section, the general assembly shall upon its organization meet in grand committee and elect some person or persons to fill the office or offices, as the case may be, for which such incapacity exists or as to which such failure to elect occurred. When the general assembly shall elect any of said officers because of the failure of any person to receive a plurality of the votes cast, the election in each case shall be made from the persons who received the same and largest number of votes.

Section 4. Temporary Appointment to Fill Vacancies in Office of Secretary of State, Attorney-General, or General Treasurer

In case of a vacancy in the office of the secretary of state, attorney-general, or general treasurer from any cause, the general assembly in grand committee shall elect some person to fill the same; provided, that if such vacancy occurs when the general assembly is not in session the governor shall appoint some person to fill such vacancy until a successor elected by the general assembly is qualified to act.

Section 5. Special Elections to Fill General Assembly Vacancies

When a senator or representative-elect shall die, remove from the state, refuse to serve, become insane, or be otherwise incapacitated, or when at an election for any senator or representative no person shall receive a plurality of the votes cast, a new election shall be held. A vacancy in the senate or house of representatives shall be filled at a new election. The general assembly shall provide by general law for the holding of such elections at such times as to insure that each town and city shall be fully represented in the general assembly during the whole of every session thereof so far as is practicable. Every person elected in accordance with this section shall hold office for the remainder of the term or for the full term, as the case may be, of the office which that person is elected to fill, and until a successor is elected and qualified.

Section 6. Elections in Grand Committee – Majority Vote – Term Of Elected Official

In elections by the general assembly in grand committee the person receiving a majority of the votes shall be elected. Every person elected by the general assembly to fill a vacancy, or pursuant to section 3 of this article, shall hold office for the remainder of the term or for the full term, as the case may be, and until a successor is elected and qualified.

Section 7. Elections in Grand Committee – Quorum – Permitted Activities

A quorum of the grand committee shall consist of a majority of all the members of the senate and a majority of all the members of the house of representatives duly assembled pursuant to an invitation from one of said bodies which has been accepted by the other, and the acceptance of which has been communicated by message to the body in which such invitation originated, and each house shall be attended by its secretaries and clerks. No act or business of any kind shall be done in grand committee other than that which is distinctly specified in the invitation by virtue of which such grand committee is assembled, except to take a recess or to dissolve; provided, that the grand committee may appoint a subcommittee of its own members to count any ballots delivered to it and report the result of such count.

Section 8. Voter Registration Lists

It shall not be necessary for the town or ward clerks to keep and transmit to the general assembly a list or register of all persons voting for general officers; but the general assembly shall have power to pass such laws on the subject as it may deem expedient.

Section 9. Reports of Campaign Contributions and Expenses

The general assembly shall require each candidate for general office in any primary, general or special election to report to the secretary of state all contributions and expenditures made by any person to or on behalf of such candidate, provided however, that the general assembly may limit such disclosure to contributions or expenditures in excess of such an amount as the general assembly shall specify.

Section 10. Limitations on Campaign Contributions – Public Financing of Campaign Expenditures of General Officers

he general assembly shall adopt limitations on all contributions to candidates for election to state and local office in any primary, general or special election and shall provide for the adoption of a plan of voluntary public financing and limitations on total campaign expenditures of campaigns for governor and such other general officers as the general assembly shall specify.

ARTICLE V: THE DISTRIBUTION OF POWERS

Section 1. Distribution of Powers

The powers of the government shall be distributed into three separate and distinct departments: the legislative, executive and judicial.

ARTICLE VI: THE LEGISLATIVE POWER

Section 1. Constitution Supreme Law of the State

This Constitution shall be the supreme law of the state, and any law inconsistent therewith shall be void. The general assembly shall pass all laws necessary to carry this Constitution into effect.

Section 2. Power Vested in General Assembly – Concurrence of Houses Required to Enact Laws – Style of Laws

The legislative power, under this Constitution, shall be vested in two houses, the one to be called the senate, the other the house of representatives; and both together the general assembly. The concurrence of the two houses shall be necessary to the enactment of laws. The style of their laws shall be, It is enacted by the general assembly as follows:

Section 3. Sessions of General Assembly – Compensation of General Assembly Members and Officers

There shall be a session of the general assembly at Providence commencing on the first Tuesday of January in each year. Commencing in January 1995, senators and representatives shall be compensated at an annual rate of ten thousand dollars ($10,000). Commencing in 1996, the rate of compensation shall be adjusted annually to reflect changes in the cost of living, as determined by the United States government during a twelve (12) month period ending in the immediately preceding year. Commencing in 2003, the president of the senate and the speaker of the house shall be compensated at an annual rate of double that of other senators and representatives.

Senators and representatives shall receive the same health insurance benefits as full-time state employees.

Senators and representatives shall be reimbursed for traveling expenses in going to and from the general assembly at the same mileage paid to state workers as of the 31st day of December in the year preceding each session.

No senator or representative shall be eligible for any pension on account of service in the general assembly after 1994; provided, however, that those senators and representatives first elected before 1994 who elect to receive compensation for legislative service in 1995 and thereafter, at the rate of five dollars ($5.00) for every day of actual attendance and eight cents (.08) per mile for traveling expenses in going to and returning from the general assembly, for a maximum of sixty (60) days in any calendar year, shall be eligible for a pension on account of service in the general assembly after 1994. The amount of such pension shall be based upon the pension program in effect for legislators on January 1, 1994.

The general assembly shall regulate the compensation of the governor and of all other officers, subject to limitations contained in the Constitution.

Section 4. Restriction on General Assembly Members Activities as Counsel

No member of the general assembly shall take any fee, or be of counsel in any case pending before either house of the general assembly, under penalty of forfeiture of seat, upon proof thereof to the satisfaction of the house in which the member sits.

Section 5. Immunities of General Assembly Members

The persons of all members of the general assembly shall be exempt from arrest and their estates from attachment in any civil action, during the session of the general assembly, and two days before the commencement and two days after the termination thereof, and all process served contrary hereto shall be void. For any speech in debate in either house, no member shall be questioned in any other place.

Section 6. Election and Qualification of General Assembly Members – Quorum and Organization of Houses

Each house shall be the judge of the elections and qualifications of its members; and a majority shall constitute a quorum to do business; but a smaller number may adjourn from day to day, and may compel the attendance of absent members in such manner, and under such penalties, as may be prescribed by such house or by law. The organization of the two houses may be regulated by law, subject to the limitations contained in this Constitution.

Section 7. Rules of houses – Contempt

Each house may determine its rules of proceeding, punish contempts, punish its members for disorderly behavior, and, with the concurrence of two-thirds, expel a member; but not a second time for the same cause.

Section 8. House Journals

Each house shall keep a journal of its proceedings. The yeas and nays of the members of either house shall, at the desire of one-fifth of those present, be entered on the journal.

Section 9. Adjournment of Houses

Neither house shall, during a session, without the consent of the other, adjourn for more that two days, nor to any other place than that in which it may be sitting.

Section 10. Continuation of Previous Powers

Repealed

Section 11. Vote Required to Pass Local or Private Appropriations

The assent of two-thirds of the members elected to each house of the general assembly shall be required to every bill appropriating the public money or property for local or private purposes.

Section 12. Property Valuations for Tax Assessments

The general assembly shall, from time to time, provide for making new valuations of property, for the assessment of taxes, in such manner as it may deem best.

Section 13. Continuance in Office Until Successors Qualify

The general assembly may provide by law for the continuance in office of any officers of election or appointment, until other persons are qualified to take their places.

Section 14. General Corporation Laws

The general assembly may provide by general law for the creation and control of corporations; provided, however, that no corporation shall be created with the power to exercise the right of eminent domain, or to acquire franchises in the streets and highways of towns and cities, except by special act of the general assembly upon a petition for the same, the pendency whereof shall be notified as may be required by law.

Section 15. Lotteries

All lotteries shall be prohibited in the state except lotteries operated by the state and except those previously permitted by the general assembly prior to the adoption of this section, and all shall be subject to the prescription and regulation of the general assembly.

Section 16. Borrowing Power of General Assembly

The general assembly shall have no powers, without the express consent of the people, to incur state debts to an amount exceeding fifty thousand dollars, except in time of war, or in case of insurrection or invasion; nor shall it in any case, without such consent, pledge the faith of the state for the payment of the obligations of others. This section shall not be construed to refer to any money that may be deposited with the state by the government of the United States.

Section 17. Borrowing in Anticipation of Receipts

Notwithstanding the provisions of section 16 of this article the general assembly may provide by law for the state to borrow in any fiscal year, in anticipation of receipts from taxes, sums of money not exceeding twenty percent of the receipts from taxes during the next prior fiscal year, and, in anticipation of receipts from other sources, additional sums of money, not exceeding ten percent of the receipts from such other sources during the said next prior fiscal year; provided, that the aggregate of all such borrowings shall not exceed a sum equal to thirty percent of the actual receipts from taxes during the said next prior fiscal year. Any money so borrowed in anticipation of such receipts shall be repaid within the fiscal year of the state in which such borrowings take place. No money shall be so borrowed in anticipation of such receipts in any fiscal year until all money so borrowed in all previous fiscal years shall have been repaid.

Section 18. Redevelopment Powers

The clearance, replanning, redevelopment, rehabilitation and improvement of blighted and substandard areas shall be a public use and purpose for which the power of eminent domain may be exercised, tax moneys and other public funds expended and public credit pledged. The general assembly may authorize cities, towns, or local redevelopment agencies to undertake and carry out projects approved by the local legislative body for such uses and purposes including the acquisition in such areas of such properties as the local legislative body may deem necessary or proper to effectuate any of the purposes of this article, although temporarily not required for such purposes, and the sale or other disposition of any such properties to private persons for private uses or to public bodies for public uses.

Section 19. Taking of Property for Highways, Streets, Places, Parks or Parkways

The general assembly may authorize the acquiring or taking in fee by the state, or by any cities or towns, of more land and property than is needed for actual construction in the establishing, laying out, widening, extending or relocating of public highways, streets, places, parks or parkways; provided, however, that the additional land and property so authorized to be acquired or taken shall be no more in extent than would be sufficient to form suitable building sites abutting on such public highway, street, place, park or parkway. After so much of the land and property has been appropriated for such public highway, street, place, park or parkway as is needed therefor, the remainder may be held and improved for any public purpose or purposes, or may be sold or leased for value with or without suitable restrictions, and in case of any such sale or lease, the person or persons from whom such remainder was taken shall have the first right to purchase or lease the same upon such terms as the state or city or town is willing to sell or lease the same.

Section 20. Local Off-Street Parking Facilities

The general assembly may authorize cities and towns to acquire property by eminent domain, or otherwise for the establishment and construction of off-street parking facilities and to maintain and operate or lease the same. Without limiting the generalities of the foregoing, any of the powers or authorities consistent with the provisions of this article for the provision of off-street parking now vested in public bodies by law, shall continue in existence and may be exercised by said public bodies, except as such powers and authorities may be modified, or repealed by the general assembly.

Section 21. Emergency Powers in Case of Enemy Attack

The general assembly, in order to insure continuity of state and local governmental operations, including the judicial functions, in periods of emergency resulting from disasters caused by enemy attack, shall have the power and the immediate duty to provide for prompt and temporary succession to the powers and duties of public offices, of whatever nature and whether filled by election or appointment, the incumbents of which may become unavailable for carrying on the powers and duties of such offices, to enact legislation permitting the convening of the general assembly at any place within or without the State of Rhode Island, and to adopt such other measures as may be necessary and proper for insuring the continuity of governmental operations during the period of said emergency. Any law enacted under this section shall apply to all cities and towns regardless of their form of charter. During said period of emergency the general assembly shall have the power to incur state debts exceeding the limitation set forth in sections 16 and 17 of this article. The powers granted and the laws enacted under this section shall not be effective after two years following the inception of an enemy attack.

Section 22. Restriction of Gambling

No act expanding the types of gambling which are permitted within the state or within any city or town therein or expanding the municipalities in which a particular form of gambling is authorized shall take effect until it has been approved by the majority of those electors voting in a statewide referendum and by the majority of those electors voting in a referendum in the municipality in which the proposed gambling would be allowed.

The secretary of state shall certify the results of the statewide referendum and the local board of canvassers of the city or town where the gambling is to be allowed shall certify the results of the local referendum to the secretary of state.

ARTICLE VII: THE HOUSE OF REPRESENTATIVES

Section 1. Composition

There shall be one hundred (100) members of the house of representatives, provided, however, that commencing in 2003 there shall be seventy-five (75) members of the house of representatives. The house of representatives shall be constituted on the basis of population and the representative districts shall be as nearly equal in population and as compact in territory as possible. The general assembly shall, after any new census taken by authority of the United States, reapportion the representation to conform to the Constitution of the state and the Constitution of the United States.

Section 2. Officers

Presiding member during organization. -- The house of representatives shall have authority to elect its speaker, clerks, and other officers. The senior member from the City of Newport, if any be present, shall preside in the organization of the house.

ARTICLE VIII: THE SENATE

Section 1. Composition

The senate shall consist of the lieutenant governor and fifty (50) members from the senatorial districts in the state, provided, however, that commencing in 2003 the senate shall consist of thirty-eight (38) members from the senatorial districts in the state. The senate shall be constituted on the basis of population and the senatorial districts shall be as nearly equal in population and as compact in territory as possible. The general assembly shall, after any new census taken by authority of the United States, reapportion the representation to conform to the Constitution of the state and the Constitution of the United States.

Section 2. Lieutenant Governor to be Presiding Officer until 2003

The lieutenant governor shall preside in the senate and in grand committee until 2003. Commencing in 2003, the senate shall elect its president, who shall preside in the senate and in grand committee, as well as its secretary and other officers from among its members and shall elect its clerks. The senior member from the city of Newport, if any be present, shall preside in the organization of the senate.

Section 3. Repealed

Section 4. Repealed

ARTICLE IX: THE EXECUTIVE POWER

Section 1. Power Vested in Governor

The chief executive power of this state shall be vested in a governor, who, together with a lieutenant governor, shall be elected by the people.

Section 2. Faithful Execution of Laws

The governor shall take care that the laws be faithfully executed.

Section 3. Captain General and Commander in Chief of Military and Navy

The governor shall be captain general and commander in chief of the military and naval forces of this state, except when they shall be called into the service of the United States.

Section 4. Reprieves

The governor shall have power to grant reprieves, after conviction, in all cases, except those of impeachment, until the end of the next session of the general assembly.

Section 5. Powers of Appointment

The governor shall, by and with the advice and consent of the senate, appoint all officers of the state whose appointment is not herein otherwise provided for and all members of any board, commission or other state or quasi-public entity which exercises executive power under the laws of this state; but the general assembly may by law vest the appointment of such inferior officers, as they deem proper, in the governor, or within their respective departments in the other general officers, the judiciary or in the heads of departments.

Section 6. Adjournment of General Assembly

In case of disagreement between the two houses of the general assembly, respecting the time or place of adjournment, certified by either, the governor may adjourn them to such time and place as the governor shall think proper; provided, that the time of adjournment shall not be extended beyond the day of the next stated session.

Section 7. Convening of Special Sessions of the General Assembly

The governor may, on extraordinary occasions, convene the general assembly at any town or city in this state, at any time not provided for by law; and in case if danger from the prevalence of epidemic or contagious disease, in the place in which the general assembly is by law to meet, or to which it may have been adjourned, or for other urgent reasons, the governor may by proclamation convene said assembly at any other place within the state.

Section 8. Commissions

All commissions shall be in the name and by authority of the State of Rhode Island and Providence Plantations; shall be sealed with the state seal, signed by the governor, and attested by the secretary.

Section 9. Vacancy in Office of Governor

If the office of the governor shall be vacant by reason of death, resignation, impeachment or inability to serve, the lieutenant governor shall shall fill the office of governor, and exercise the powers and authority appertaining thereto, until a governor is qualified to act, or until the office is filled at the next election.

Section 10. Vacancies in Both Offices of Governor and Lieutenant Governor

If the offices of governor and lieutenant governor be both vacant by reason of death, resignation, impeachment, or inability to serve, the speaker of the house of representatives shall in like manner fill the office of governor during such vacancy.

Section 11. Compensation of Governor and Lieutenant Governor

The compensation of the governor and lieutenant governor shall be established by law, and shall not be diminished during the term for which they are elected.

Section 12. Powers and Duties of Secretary, Attorney-General, and General Treasurer

The duties and powers of the secretary, attorney-general and general treasurer shall be the same under this Constitution as are now established, or as from time to time may be prescribed by law.

Section 13. Pardons

The governor, by and with the advice and consent of the senate, shall hereafter exclusively exercise the pardoning power, except in cases of impeachment, to the same extent as such power is now exercised by the general assembly.

Section 14. Veto Power of Governor

Veto overrides by general assembly

Acts effective without action by governor. -- Every bill, resolution, or vote (except such as relate to adjournment, the organization or conduct of either or both houses of the general assembly, and resolutions proposing amendment to the Constitution) which shall have passed both houses of the general assembly shall be presented to the governor. If the governor approve it the governor shall sign it, and thereupon it shall become operative, but if the governor does not approve it the governor shall return it, accompanied by the governor's objections in writing to the house in which it originated, which shall enter the governor's objections in full upon its journal and proceed to reconsider it. If, after such reconsideration, three-fifths of the members present and voting in that house shall vote to pass the measure, it shall be sent with the objections, to the other house, by which it shall likewise by reconsidered, and if approved by three-fifths of the members present and voting in that house, it shall become operative in the same manner as if the governor had approved it, but in such cases the votes of both houses shall be determined by ayes and nays and the names of the members voting for and against the measure shall be entered upon the journal of each house, respectively. If the measure shall not be returned by the governor within six days (Sundays excepted) after it shall have been presented to the governor the same shall become operative unless the general assembly, by adjournment, prevents its return, in which case it shall become operative unless transmitted by the governor nor to the secretary of state, with the governor's disapproval in writing within ten days after such adjournment.

Section 15. State budget

The governor shall prepare and present to the general assembly an annual, consolidated operating and capital improvement state budget.

Section 16. Limitation on State Spending. [Effective July 1,2007 until July 1, 2012]

(a) No appropriation, supplemental appropriation or budget act shall cause the aggregate state general revenue appropriations enacted in any given fiscal year to exceed ninety-eight percent (98%) of the estimated state general revenues for such fiscal year from all sources, including estimated unencumbered general revenues to the new fiscal year remaining at the end of the previous fiscal year. Estimated unencumbered general revenues are calculated by taking the estimated general revenue cash balance at the end of the fiscal year less estimated revenue anticipation bonds or notes, estimated general revenue encumbrances, estimated continuing general revenue appropriations and the amount of the budget reserve account at the end of said fiscal year.

(b) The amount between the applicable percentage in (a) and one hundred percent (100%) of the estimated state general revenue for any fiscal year as estimated in accordance with subsection (a) of this section shall be appropriated in any given fiscal year into the budget reserve account; provided, however, that no such payment will be made which would increase the total of the budget reserve account to more than three percent (3%) of only the estimated state general revenues as set by subsection (a) of this section. In the event that the payment to be made into the budget reserve account would increase the amount in said account to more than three percent (3%) of estimated state general revenues that said amount shall be transferred to the Rhode Island Capital Plan fund to be used solely for funding capital projects.

(c) Within forty-five (45) days after the close of any fiscal year, all unencumbered general revenue in the year end surplus account from the said fiscal year shall be transferred to the general fund.

Section 16. Limitation on State Spending

(a) No appropriation, supplemental appropriation or budget act shall cause the aggregate state general revenue appropriations enacted in any given fiscal year to exceed ninety seven percent (97%) of the estimated state general revenues for such fiscal year from all sources, including estimated unencumbered general revenues to the new fiscal year remaining at the end of the previous fiscal year. Estimated unencumbered general revenues are calculated by taking the estimated general revenue cash balance at the end of the fiscal year less estimated revenue anticipation bonds or notes, estimated general revenue encumbrances, estimated continuing general revenue appropriations and the amount of the budget reserve account at the end of said fiscal year.

(b) The amount between the applicable percentage in (a) and one hundred percent (100%) of the estimated state general revenue for any fiscal year as estimated in accordance with subsection (a) of this section shall be appropriated in any given fiscal year into the budget reserve account; provided, however, that no such payment will be made which would increase the total of the budget reserve account to more than five percent (5%) of only the estimated state general revenues as set by subsection (a) of this section. In the event that the payment to be made into the budget reserve account would increasec the total of the budget reserve account to more than five percent (5%) of only the estimated state general revenues as set by subsection (1) of this section. In the event that the payment to be made into the budget reserve account would increase the amount in said account to more than five percent (5%) of estimated state general revenues that said amount shall be transferred to the Rhode Island Capital Plan fund to be used solely for funding capital projects.

(c) Within forty-five (45) days after the close of any fiscal year, all unencumbered general revenue in the year end surplus account from the said fiscal year shall be transferred to the general fund.

Section 17. Budget Reserve Account

There is hereby established a budget reserve account within the general fund. Revenues in this budget reserve account may be appropriated in the event of an emergency involving the health, safety or welfare of the citizens of the state of Rhode Island or in the event of an unanticipated deficit in any given fiscal year, such appropriations to be approved by a majority vote of each house of the general assembly.

ARTICEL X: JUDICIAL POWER

Section 1. Power Vested in Court

The judicial power of this state shall be vested in one supreme court, and in such inferior courts as the general assembly may, from time to time, ordain and establish.

Section 2. Jurisdiction of Supreme and Inferior Courts

Quorum of supreme court. -- The supreme court shall have final revisory and appellate jurisdiction upon all questions of law and equity. It shall have power to issue prerogative writs, and shall also have such other jurisdiction as may, from time to time, by prescribed by law. A majority of its judges shall always be necessary to constitute a quorum. The inferior courts shall have such jurisdiction as may, from time to time, be prescribed by law.

Section 3. Advisory Opinions By Supreme Court

The judges of the supreme court shall give their written opinion upon any question of law whenever requested by the governor or by either house of the general assembly.

Section 4. State Court Judges – Judicial Selection

The governor shall fill any vacancy of any justice of the Rhode Island Supreme Court by nominating, on the basis of merit, a person from a list submitted by an independent non-partisan judicial nominating commission, and by and with the advice and consent of the senate, and by and with the separate advice and consent of the house of representatives, shall appoint said person as a justice of the Rhode Island Supreme Court. The governor shall fill any vacancy of any judge of the Rhode Island Superior Court, Family Court, District, Workers' Compensation Court, Administrative Adjudication Court, or any other state court which the general assembly may from time to time establish by nominating on the basis of merit, a person from a list submitted by the aforesaid judicial nominating commission, and by and with the advice and consent of the senate, shall appoint said person to the court where the vacancy occurs. The powers, duties, and composition of the judicial nominating commission shall be defined by statute.

Section 5. Tenure of Supreme Court Justices

Justices of the supreme court shall hold office during good behavior.

Section 6. Judges of Supreme Court – Compensation

The judges of the supreme court shall receive a compensation for their services, which shall not be diminished during their continuance in office.

Section 7. Wardens and Justices of the Peace

The towns of New Shoreham and Jamestown may continue to elect their wardens as heretofore. The other towns and the city of Providence may elect such number of justices of the peace, resident therein, as they may deem proper. The jurisdiction of said justices and wardens shall be regulated by law. The justices shall be commissioned by the governor.

ARTICLE XI: IMPEACHMENTS

Section 1. Power to Impeach – Procedure

Suspension from office impeachment. -- The house of representatives shall have the sole power of impeachment. A resolution of impeachment shall not be considered unless it is signed by one-quarter (1/4) of the members. For the purposes of impeachment, the general assembly and committees thereof shall have the power to compel the attendance of witnesses and production of documents. A vote of two-thirds (2/3) of the members shall be required for an impeachment of the governor. Any officer impeached shall thereby be suspended from the office until judgment in the case shall have been pronounced.

Section 2. Trial of Impeachments

All impeachments shall be tried by the senate; and when sitting for that purpose, they shall be under oath or affirmation. No person shall be convicted except by vote of two-thirds of the members elected. When the governor is impeached, the chief or presiding justice of the supreme court, for the time being, shall preside, with a casting vote in all preliminary questions.

Section 3. Officers Subject to Impeachment -- Grounds and Effect of Conviction

The governor and all other executive and judicial officers shall be liable to impeachment. The governor or any other executive officer shall be removed from office if, upon impeachment, such officer shall be found incapacitated or guilty of the commission of a felony or crime of moral turpitude, misfeasance or malfeasance in office. Judges shall be removed if, upon impeachment, they shall be found incapacitated or guilty of the commission of a felony or crime of moral turpitude, misfeasance or malfeasance in office or violation of the canons of judicial ethics. Judgment of incapacity or guilt in a case of impeachment shall not extend further than to removal from office. The person convicted shall, nevertheless, be liable to indictment, trial and punishment, according to laws.

ARTICLE XII: EDUCATION

Section 1. Duty of General Assembly to Promote Schools and Libraries

The diffusion of knowledge, as well as of virtue among the people, being essential to the preservation of their rights and liberties, it shall be the duty of the general assembly to promote public schools and public libraries, and to adopt all means which it may deem necessary and proper to secure to the people the advantages and opportunities of education and public library services.

Section 2. Perpetual School Fund

The money which now is or which may hereafter be appropriated by law for the establishment of a permanent fund for the support of public schools, shall be securely invested and remain a perpetual fund for that purpose.

Section 3. Donations

All donations for the support of public schools, or for other purposes of education, which may be received by the general assembly, shall be applied according to the terms prescribed by the donors.

Section 4. Implementation of Article

Diversion of funds prohibited. -- The general assembly shall make all necessary provisions by law for carrying this article into effect. It shall not divert said money or fund from the aforesaid uses, nor borrow, appropriate, or use the same, or any part thereof, for any other purpose, under any pretense whatsoever.

ARTICLE XIII: HOME RULE FOR CITIES AND TOWNS

Section 1. Intent of Article

It is the intention of this article to grant and confirm to the people of every city and town in this state the right of self government in all local matters.

Section 2. Local Legislative Powers

Every city and town shall have the power at any time to adopt a charter, amend its charter, enact and amend local laws relating to its property, affairs and government not inconsistent with this constitution and laws enacted by the general assembly in conformity with the powers reserved to the general assembly.

Section 3. Local Legislative Bodies

Notwithstanding anything contained in this article, every city and town shall have a legislative body composed of one or two branches elected by vote of its qualified electors.

Section 4. Powers of General Assembly Over Cities and Towns

The general assembly shall have the power to act in relation to the property, affairs and government of any city or town by general laws which shall apply alike to all cities and towns, but which shall not affect the form of government of any city or town. The general assembly shall also have the power to act in relation to the property, affairs and government of a particular city or town provided that such legislative action shall become effective only upon approval by a majority of the qualified electors of the said city or town voting at a general or special election, except that in the case of acts involving the imposition of a tax or the expenditure of money by a town the same shall provide for the submission thereof to those electors in said town qualified to vote upon a proposition to impose a tax or for the expenditure of money.

Section 5. Local Taxing and Borrowing Powers

Nothing contained in this article shall be deemed to grant to any city or town the power to levy, assess and collect taxes or to borrow money, except as authorized by the general assembly.

Section 6. Charter Commissions

Every city and town shall have the power to adopt a charter in the following manner: Whenever a petition for the adoption of a charter signed by fifteen percent of the qualified electors of a city, or in a town by fifteen percent, but not less than one hundred in number, of those persons qualified to vote on any proposition to impose a tax or for the expenditure of money shall be filed with the legislative body of any city or town the same shall be referred forthwith to the canvassing authority which shall within ten days after its receipt determine the sufficiency thereof and certify the results to the legislative body of said city or town. Within sixty days thereafter the legislative body of a city shall submit to its qualified electors and the legislative body of a town shall submit to the electors of said town qualified to vote upon a proposition to impose a tax or for the expenditure of money the following question: "Shall a commission be appointed to frame a charter?" and the legislative body of any city or town shall provide by ordinance or resolution a method for the nomination and election of a charter commission to frame a charter consisting in a city of nine qualified electors and in a town of nine electors of said town qualified to vote upon a proposition to impose a tax or for the expenditure of money who shall be elected at large without party or political designation and who shall be listed alphabetically on the ballot used for said election. Such ordinance or resolution shall provide for the submission of the question and the election of the charter commission at the same time. Upon approval of the question submitted the nine candidates who individually receive the greater number of votes shall be declared elected and shall constitute the charter commission.

Section 7. Adoption of Charters

Within one year from the date of the election of the charter commission the charter framed by the commission shall be submitted to the legislative body of the city or town which body shall provide for publication of said charter and shall provide for the submission of said charter to the electors of a city or town qualified to vote for general state officers at the general election next succeeding thirty days from the date of the submission of the charter by the charter commission. If said charter is approved by a majority of said electors voting thereon, it shall become effective upon the date fixed therein.

Section 8. Amendments to Charters

The legislative body of any city or town may propose amendments to a charter which amendments shall be submitted for approval in the same manner as provided in this article for the adoption of a charter except that the same may be submitted at a special election, and provided further that in the case of a town, amendments concerning a proposition to impose a tax or for the expenditure of money, shall be submitted at a special or regular financial town meeting.

Section 9. Filing of Charter Petitions to Bicameral Legislative Bodies

Whenever the legislative body of any city or town consists of more than one branch, a petition for the adoption of a charter as provided in this article may be filed with either branch of said legislative body.

Section 10. Charter certificates – Signing – Recordation – Deposit – Judicial notice

Duplicate certificates shall be made setting forth the charter adopted and any amendments approved and the same shall be signed by a majority of the canvassing authority; one of such certified copies shall be deposited in the office of the secretary of state and the other after having been recorded in the records of the city or town shall be deposited among the archives of the said city or town and all courts shall take judicial notice thereof.

Section 11. Judicial Powers Unaffected by Article

The judicial powers of the state shall not be diminished by the provisions of this article.

ARTICLE XIV: CONSTITUTIONAL AMENDMENTS AND REVISIONS

Section 1. Procedure for Proposing and Approving Amendments

The general assembly may propose amendments to the constitution of the state by a roll call vote of a majority of the members elected to each house. Any amendment thus proposed shall be published in such manner as the general assembly shall direct, and submitted to the electors at the next general election as provided in the resolution of approval; and, if then approved by a majority of the electors voting thereon, it shall become a part of the constitution.

Section 2. Constitutional Conventions

The general assembly, by a vote of a majority of the members elected to each house, may at any general election submit the question, "Shall there be a convention to amend or revise the constitution?" to the qualified electors of the state. If the question be not submitted to the people at some time during any period of ten years, the secretary of state shall submit it at the next general election following said period. Prior to a vote by the qualified electors on the holding of a convention, the general assembly, or the governor if the general assembly fails to act, shall provide for a bi-partisan preparatory commission to assemble information on constitutional questions for the electors. If a majority of the electors voting at such election on said question shall vote to hold a convention, the general assembly at its next session shall provide by law for the election of delegates to such convention. The number of delegates shall be equal to the number of members of the house of representatives and shall be apportioned in the same manner as the members of the house of representatives. No revision or amendment of this constitution agreed upon by such convention shall take effect until the same has been submitted to the electors and approved by a majority of those voting thereon.

ARTICLE XV: GENERAL TRANSITION

Section 1. Rights and Duties of Public Bodies Unaffected –
Continuation of Laws, Ordinances, Regulations and Rules

The rights and duties of all public bodies shall remain as if this
constitution had not been adopted with the exception of such
changes as are contained in this constitution. All laws,
ordinances, regulations and rules of court not contrary to, or
inconsistent with, the provisions of this constitution shall remain
in force, until they shall expire by their own limitation or shall be
altered or repealed pursuant to this constitution.

Section 2. Validity of Bonds, Debts, Contracts, Suits, Actions,
and Rights of Actions Continued

The validity of all public and private bonds, debts and contracts,
and of all suits, actions, and rights of action, shall continue as if
no change had taken place.

Section 3. Continuation of Office Holders

All officers filling any office by election or appointment shall
continue the duties thereof, until the end of the terms to which
they were appointed or elected, and until their offices shall have
been abolished or their successors elected and qualified in
accordance with this constitution or laws enacted pursuant
thereto.

Section 4. Implementing Legislation for Article III, Sections 7
and 8, and Article IV, section 10

On or before June 1, 1988, the general assembly shall adopt
implementing legislation for article III, sections 7 and 8, and for
article IV, section 10.